October

Cyprus Poems

David Jaffin

October
Cyprus Poems

First published in the United Kingdom in 2021 by
Shearsman Books
50 Westons Hill Drive
Emersons Green
Bristol BS16 7DF

Shearsman Books Ltd Registered Office
30–31 St. James Place, Mangotsfield, Bristol BS16 9JB
(this address not for correspondence)

www.shearsman.com

978-1-84861-402-4

Distributed for Shearsman Books in the U. S. A.
by Small Press Distribution, 1341 Seventh Avenue, Berkeley, CA 94710
E-Mail orders@spdbooks.org
www.spdbooks.org

.

Production, composition, & cover design: Edition Wortschatz,
a service of Neufeld Verlag, Cuxhaven/Germany
E-Mail info@edition-wortschatz.de, www.edition-wortschatz.de

Title illustration:
"La Barque mystique" (The Mystical Boat), undated
by Odilon Redon (1840–1916)
Pastel, 51 × 63,5 cm. Collection Andrea Woodner
Source: akg-images

Printed in Germany

Contents

Part 1

Cyprus (5) 21
A moonful (3) 23
Comforting (3) 24
That tiny (2) 25
Cyprus may (4) 25
Many little (4) 27
Two Mary (6)............28
At least (2) 30
Here in Cy (3)...........31
Even though (2) 32
This sea' (2) 33
Reflection.................33
Tiny sparr 34
At the sea..................34
Phantomed (2) 35
That so-thor (2) 35
It's not 36
A walking (2) 36
Answering (3) 37
One poem (3) 38
Have the (5) 38
Our special (3) 40
Absent-mind (2)........41
"Children' (3) 42

This Sunday (4)........43
A spotted 44
This early (2).............44
Working (2) 45
Cruising (3) 46
Multi-talen (2) 47
Dollar and.................47
The cruise (2) 48
Getting too 48
2nd Round (2)............49
If the eye (3).............50
Most half- (2)............51
When the (2)............52
Are the wave (3) 53
If it's (2) 54
Leafless si 54
That straw (3) 55
When can (3) 56
Finely express (2)........57
If the Turk (4) 58
Has that well (2)........59
Other direct (3).........60
He a middle- (3)........61
Sea-timed (3) 62
Does the (2) 63
Why do (2) 64

She remain (3)...........64
Early even 65
He dream..................65
Usually (3) 66
For some (3)..............67
It remain (3)...............68
What kind of (3)........69
This island' (2) 70
Americana (7) 71
There are (9) 73
Even at 7:30 76
Tradition (3) 76
Are most cat' (2)........77
It wasn't (3)...............78
Low-level..................79
"The Legend" (4)......80
The ever- (4).............81
This will (4) 82
Even though (3) 83
Those rand (2) 84
Critics who (3)..........85
Our two (6) 86
One must be (4)........88
We paint (5) 89
Fall in (3) 91
The older (3).............92
The sea' (3) 93
When indoor 94

The who is (3)...........95
It had be (3) 96
I speak too (3) 97
The prevail (3) 98
If life's (2)..................99
Mooned (2).............100
He towering (2) 101
I've never (3) 102
Extreme (2).............103
Our turtler (3).........104
These sunny (4) 105
Paradise (3) 106
False or (2) 107
Curtain (2)..............108
My mother (4) 109
Early morn (3).........110
I've never (3) 111
Everything' (2) 112
Stern-look (3) 113
Answering John 114
Mooned? (3) 115
Garcilaso' (2)...........116
The waves (3)..........117
Walking-the- (3) 118
First scanty (2).........119
On and off (8) 120
Early morn (3).........122
Why these (3)..........123

Tiny flie (2) 124

"Inextinguishable" .. 125

How often (4) 127

If love' (2) 128

If what (2) 129

Why did (5) 130

Annulled? (4) 131

When the (2) 132

Steven Forster (2) 133

The sea' (3) 134

Flag waving (4) 135

Most diffi (4) 136

Sparrows (4) 137

Friday's (2) 138

Do Bikini (3) 139

Why those (3) 140

Weimar on (4) 141

The spirit (5) 142

Rather ugly (3) 143

There have (3) 144

What should- (2) 145

Is it (3) 146

When I (3) 147

He's the (2) 148

It's diffi (5) 148

What one (3) 150

One should (4) 151

Shakespear (4) 152

Unforget (3) 153

Should one (3) 154

Up today (3) 155

One must (3) 156

Does history 157

One can't (4) 158

Those barren (3) 159

Merkel o (2) 160

Two-timed (3) 161

The Annun (4) 162

Arthur Racham- 163

Terracing 163

The aband 164

The Troodoos (4) 165

Savas our (3)   166

No one (5) 167

Rosemarie (5) 168

The spider' (2) 169

The sea (3) 170

Blue (2) 171

When these (4) 172

Letter-writ (3) 173

Because of (2) 174

These soft (2) 175

Some of (3) 176

"They're just (2) 177

Waiting for (3) 178

One dead (2) 179

An even- (2)............ 180

He built his (4)........ 181

Cyprus so (4) 182

"Handwrit (4).......... 183

Our taxi (6) 184

Perhaps (5)............... 185

It took (4) 187

"He (Savas) (4) 188

Few tourist (3) 189

The continu (3)....... 190

This still (3) 191

Tourism (4)............. 192

That walled (3)........ 193

Fewer and few (4).... 194

When Europe' (3) ... 195

That late-vin (3) 196

Some of (2) 197

The water' (2) 198

Open-borders (3) 199

We've now (4).........200

Beach-comb (3) 201

Savas' cat (4)............202

This newly (3).........203

Life must (3) 204

The tourist (4).........205

Some hear (7)..........206

Such a vast (3) 208

That last- (6)...........209

Cyprus has be (3) 211

Rarely if e (4).......... 212

Something (4) 213

Have Aron (4) 214

One can't (3)........... 215

Despite (4) 216

P. S. These wind...... 217

Are cloud (3)........... 218

Clouding- (3).......... 219

Are we leav (4) 220

I imagine (2) 221

Are these (3) 222

Poetry Book 106 225

Part 2:

Other earlier Poems

If you're a (4)...........227

Dance of (2) 228

It became im (4)......229

My curtain..............230

Our still (3) 231

They needn't (2) 232

She'd had (6)...........232

Without a (3) 234

After 13 (3) 235

How far must (3).....236

She learned (3) 237
Differing per (5) 238
Is this sky (4) 240
If the bible' (3) 241
It may have (3) 242
Ship of fools (8) 243
First not (3) 245
He remained (2) 246
Our dean (3) 247
It's become (2) 248
All's normal (3) 249
Women disap (2) 250
That take-it (2) 251
Teaching (3) 252
My two-sided (3) 253
If Rosemarie (3) 254
If marriage (3) 255
If you listen (5) 256
Never having (4) 258
One named (3)........259
These split- (2)........260
With her (4) 261
An abandon (4) 262
Why have mir 263
Locked (4) 264
"Just call (2) 265
Two ways Two (7) ...266
The children' (2) 268

Has poetry' (4) 269
It usually (4) 270
It remain (4) 271
The American (4)....272
Compromise (4)......273
Is the Japan (4) 274
If keeping- (2) 275
He as many (4) 276
Do the hard- (2) 277
Handle-with (3) 278
For Hanni our (2)....279
The little (2)............280
Fake or real (4) 280
These almost 282
Raw weather' (2).....282
Elgar's (3)................283
Torrential (2)...........284
Womanliness (3) 285
If I were a (3)...........286
Most men be (3)......287
Poems or (3) 288
Some person (3) 289
A big cele (4)...........290
These wind (3)........291
Haydn's early (3) 292
Bunched (2)............293
If at time (2) 294
Wind-Phantom 295

9

We didn't (5)...........296

Why I so (5)............297

If he's pre (3)...........299

Time's now (3)........300

Few painter (2)........301

Our rather (2).........302

I can hard (2)...........303

Each time (2)..........304

Others as (4)...........305

How easily (4).........306

Writing poem 307

That special (5).......308

If animal' (2)...........309

Why one must (2)...310

Macke succeed........310

Waiting' (4).............311

The so under- (6)....312

Eve's little................314

To-be-locked (5).....314

Judging art (4).........316

All in the (4)...........318

If "my poetry' (8)....319

Facts and fig (4).......321

Reading my (4).......322

The most un (3)......323

Women are (3)........324

No one....................325

After the (6)............326

Can one recog (5)....328

Did (2)....................329

Pantheism (2)..........330

Sometime (4)..........331

Having been (2)......332

Dog-walker (3).......333

Why should (2).......334

*Poetry books
by David Jaffin 335*

With continuing thanks for
Marina Moisel
preparing
this manuscript

and to Hanni Bäumler
for her well-placed
photograph

If I had to classify my poetry, it could best be done through the classical known "saying the most by using the least". The aim is thereby set: transparency, clarity, word-purity. Every word must carry its weight in the line and the ultimate aim is a unity of sound, sense, image and idea. Poetry, more than any other art, should seek for a unity of the senses, as the French Symbolists, the first poetic modernists, realized through the interchangeability of the senses: "I could hear the colors of her dress." One doesn't hear colors, but nevertheless there is a sensual truth in such an expression.

Essential is "saying the most by using the least". Compression is of the essence. And here are some of my most personal means of doing so turning verbs into nouns and the reverse, even within a double-context "Why do the leaves her so ungenerously behind". Breaking words into two or even three parts to enable both compression and the continuing flow of meaning. Those words must be placed back together again, thereby revealing their inner structure-atomising.

One of my critics rightly said: "Jaffin's poetry is everywhere from one seemingly unrelated poem to the next." Why? Firstly because of my education and interests trained at New York University as a cultural and intellectual historian. My doctoral dissertation on historiography emphasizes the necessary historical continuity. Today we often judge the past with the mind and mood of the present, totally contrary to their own historical context. I don't deny the past-romanticism and classical but integrate them within a singular modern context of word-usage and sensibility. Musically that would place me within the "classical-romantic tradition" of Haydn, Mozart, Mendelssohn, Brahms and Nielsen but at the very modern end of that tradition.

My life historically is certainly exceptional. My father was a prominent New York Jewish lawyer. The law never interested me, but history always did. A career as a cultural-intellectual historian was mine-for-the-asking, but I rejected historical relativism. That led me to a marriage with a devout German lady – so I took to a calling of Jesus-the-Jew in post-Auschwitz Germany. For ca. two decades I wrote and lectured all over Germany on Jesus the Jew. Thereby my knowledge and understanding of both interlocked religions became an essential part of my being. History, faith and religion two sides of me but also art, classical music and literature were of essential meaning – so many poems on poetry, classical music and painting.

Then Rosemarie and I have been very happily married for 60 years now. Impossible that a German and Jew could be so happily married so shortly after the war? I've written love poems for her, hundreds and hundreds over those 60 years, not only the love poems, as most are, of the first and often unfulfilling passion, but "love and marriage go together like a horse and carriage". Perhaps too prosaic for many poets?

When did I become a poet? My sister Lois wrote reasonably good poetry as an adolescent. I, only interested in sports until my Bar Mitzvah, a tournament tennis and table-tennis player, coached baseball and basketball teams, also soccer.

My sister asked whether I'd ever read Dostoyevsky. I'd only read John R. Tunis sports books and the sports section of the *New York Times* so I answered "in which sports was he active?" She said, rather condescendingly, "If you haven't read Dostoyevsky, you haven't lived." So I went to the library for the very first time and asked for a book by this Dostoyevsky. I received *Poor People*, his first book, that made him world famous. My mother shocked to see me reading and most especially a book about poor people said, "David, don't read that it will make you sad, unhappy – we, living in Scarsdale, weren't after all, poor people. From there it went quickly to my Tolstoy, Hardy and so on. In music it started with the hit parade, then *Lost in the Stars*, then the popular classics and with 15 or 16 my Haydn, Mozart, Schütz, Victoria ... And then at Ann Arbor and NYU to my artists, most especially Giovanni Bellini, Van der Weyden, Georges de la Tour, Corot and Gauguin ...

But it was Wallace Stevens' reading in the early 50s in the YMHA that set me off – he didn't read very well, but his 13 Ways of Looking at a Blackbird, Idea of Order at Key West, Two Letters (in *Poems Posthumous*), Peter Quince at the Clavier, The Snowman ... and the excellent obituary in *Time* magazine plus the letter he answered some of my poems with compliments but "you must be your own hardest critic". That pre-determined my extremely self-critical way with a poem. Please don't believe that prolific means sloppy, for I'm extremely meticulous with each and every poem.

My poems were published in the order written and I'm way ahead of any counting … The poem is a dialogical process as everything in life. The words come to me not from me, and if they strike or possibly join-a-union then I become desparate, read long-winded poets like Paz to set me off – he's very good at odd times. Those poems need my critical mood-mind as much as I need their very specially chosen words – not the "magic words" of the romantics, but the cleansed words of Jaffin – Racine used only 500 words. My words too are a specially limited society, often used, but in newly-felt contexts.

O something very special: I have a terrible poetic memory. If I had a good one as presumably most poets, I'd write say one poem about a butterfly, and every time I see/saw a butterfly it would be that one, that poem. But I forget my poems, so each butterfly, lizard, squirrel … is other-placed, other-mooded, other-worded, other-Jaffined. That's the main reason why I am most certainly the most prolific of all poets.

Shakespeare is the greatest of us: his sonnets live most from the fluency and density of his language. I advise all future poets to keep away from his influence and the poetic greatness of The Bible.

Yours truly
David Jaffin

P. S.: As a preacher the truth (Christ) should become straight-lined, timelessly so, but as a poet it's quite different. What interests me most are those contradictions which live deeply within all of us, not only in theory, but daily in the practice. And then the romantics have led me to those off-sided thoroughly poetic truths that mysteriously not knowing where that darkened path will lead us.

Poetry Book 106

Part 1

.

Cyprus (5)

a) *voted two gener*

ations ago

to become a
part of Greece

b) *first time in*

over 1,000 year

s Next generat
ion. "Greek Cyp

riotes" the
younger ones sim

c) *ply Cypriote*

s Identity

changes because
of historical

use the Austr

d) ians aren't Ger

mans the East
Germans remain

for a good part
East Germans

Who am I

e) neither German

nor American
Rosemarie's

my undisclosed
identity.

A moonful (3)

a) night over the

Aegean Sea

our time-sus
pending view

b) shadows us

from other

star-lit
causes while

the distant ex

c) pressive wave

s dialo
gues repeti

tive unanswer
ing-question

s.

Comforting (3)

a) for aging per

sons trans

lates at best
with a soft

b) reclining

seat at the

water's edge
to a trans

forming view
of contempla

c) ing thought

s reaching-out

even to the
horizon's dis

tancing.

That tiny *(2)*

a) tot-of-a-boy

throwing e

ven tinier
pebbles into

a watering
dialogue of

b) I'm trying

to tell you

what really
matters at

the very
least for

me-now.

Cyprus may *(4)*

a) not yet appear

on your in

creasing
ly extending

b) vacation-

list but those

bodily ful
filling swim–

days and the

c) island's legion

s of wondrous
Byzantine

churches and
monasterie

d) s shouldn'

t be missed

if only for
your eye's

and soul's
sake.

Many little (4)

a) children

seem to be

lieve that
big hats make

b) big person

s That's per

haps why
they love wear

ing over-siz

c) ed hats that

seem to expand
their self-en

dowing imagin
ations Is

d) Trump's "Ameri

ca First" hat

transmitting
much the same

message.

Two Mary *(6)*

a) s of the Ro

man Catholic

Church the
one young beau

b) tified as the

infant Jesus'

mother The o
ther the matron

ly mother-of-

c) the-church Do

they appear
so different

ly but act
ually remain

d) the same at

different

ages–level
s The way a

woman sees a

e) nother woman

and through
men's other

wise eyes

f) almost as if

they've been
transformed

into a separate
identity.

At least (2)

a) most American

s understand

"He's having
a field day"

but the ex
pression it

b) self rarely

clues us its

eventful
meaning Why

field what
field.

Here in Cy *(3)*

a) prus one still

marries a

family not
only a person

In America

b) and Germany

that's often
quite other

wise Is that
progress or

does it

c) signify the

break-down of

a tradition
al and self-

protective
family–sense.

Even though (2)

   a) the Greeks

   fought to pro

   tect Cyprus
   against the

   Turkish invad
   ers still the

   b) Cypriotes con

   tinued to

   feel more and
   more the inde

   pendent nation
   they'd actual

   ly become.

This sea' (2)

a) s surround

ing my thought

s with a
wealth of con

templative
wave-length–

b) imagining

s No one

and nothing'
s overhear

ing our self–
intuning dia

logue.

Reflection

s through
glass leave

the impress
ion of hav

ing seen
more than

what's act
ually signi

fying–it
self.

Tiny sparr

ows dotting
the surface

of these
sandied shore

s with their
impulsive

foot-find
ing time-

reach.

At the sea

side it's the
varied plea

sure boats
that set the

measure to
my eye-sens

ing time-dis
tancing

s.

Phantomed (2)

a) First time

I've witness

ed an unman
ned drone

scanning

b) the pleasur

able shore
s of this

peaceable
post-Grac

ean island.

That so-thor (2)

a) oughly over-pro

portioned
grandma im

pression
ed an expan

b) sive-certain

ty of old–

world protect
ive-comfort

ings.

It's not

only the seen
but the thought-

seen that im
pression

s my sensi
tive timely

out-reaching
poetic-pro

cessing
s.

A walking (2)

a) skeletal

length-of-a

man on this
lifeful late

afternoon
Cypriotic

b) beach impress

ioned a warning

(perhaps meant
for me) which

I simply re
fused to de

cipher.

Answering *(3)*

a) S. L. Here in

Cyprus in

October the
days all sun

shine and

b) the sky's

all blue while
the moon de

cides its ti
dal magnetic-

pull reclaim

c) ing after those

first human
moon-steps

its romant
ic poetic-per

sonality.

One poem *(3)*

  a) leads to the

  next as one

  day follows a
  nother They'

  b) ve all been

  called and

  patiently
  await as

  hungried school

  c) children their

  own predetermin
  ed turn in that

  anxiously ex
  tending-line.

Have the *(5)*

  a) best of drama

  s and novel

  s become an
  alternate

b) means of depth

ening our know

ledge of hu
man behavior

or should we

c) depend more

on our own
intuitive

reflective
ness Least

d) of all espec

ially exampl

ed through
Freud those

e) less than his

torically

and sociolog
ically-based

psychologist
s.

Our special (3)

a) hotel with

the panoram

ic view of
the Aegean

b) Sea shaping

more than my

own poetic
scope could

possibly

c) hold and even

of Altdorfer'
s Alexander'

s epic battle–
scene.

Absent-mind (2)

a) *ed could in*

some cases be

conceived
as a compli

ments–of–
sorts imply

b) *ing he or*

she possess

es a mind
that could

actually
take–leave

from itself.

"Children' (3)

a) s games" Breugh
el calls them
while child
ren are gamed–

b) enough in them
selves explora
tively sens
ing of most
all touched

c) seen and exam
plified in
their own spec
ial sort-of-
way.

This Sunday (4)

a) beaches' plural

ity of little

girls of that
2 or 3 year

b) old vintage

trying as

best as they
possibly could

to imitate
their mother'

c) s grown up

sense of-com

posure while
playful in

stincts still

d) mostly pre-de

termined their
what's now

and what's
wherefore.

A spotted

leopard-like
cat jungled

my mind in
to an episod

ic time's-
away-reach

from that
species indig

enous fear-
of-water.

This early (2)

a) departed Oct

ober beach

by 4pm seem
s already pre

paring for the
lonliness

b) of the moon'

s desolately

reviving wave-
extending

autumnal even
ing-call.

Working (2)

a) daily in the

mines they

came to real
ise the depth

of darkness

b) not only out

side but pene
trating the

depths of
their very-be

ing.

Cruising (3)

a) Cyprian shore

s these undu

lating hills
began reestab

b) lishing them

selves as in

delible time
less land–

markings
while we be

c) gan to extend

with their rhy

thmically
self-defin

ing explora
tions.

Multi-talen *(2)*

a) ted person

s as our

cruise–owner
have difficul

ty identify
ing the where

b) and what of

their essent

ial–being
elusive

ly self–deter
mining.

Dollar and

cent thinker
s as my fa

ther helped
birth a word

and meaning
poet much of

the same sort
though no more

worth than a
penny-a-line.

The cruise (2)

a) owner while

pointing-out

the sights
to my attent

ive Rosemarie
expressing

b) himself finger

and hand-wise

much as an i
tinerant pre

acher or high
school teacher.

Getting too

used to fact
s and figure

s leaves a
deepening di

vide from
what's multi-

implied poet
ically-sens

ed.

2nd *Round (2)*

a) of Corona slow-

down more than

half-empty
hotels and rest

aurants as if

b) phantomed

with the ghost
s of a still-

persisting e
ver-present

past.

If the eye (3)

a) doesn't see

the poem can'

t word it
or is it the

b) other way-

round If the

poem doesn'
t word the

eye can't

c) see Both way

s predeter
mine a dialogi

cal-together
ness.

Most half- *(2)*

a) grown boys re

main at the

very least
potencial row

dies Fun's the
name of their

b) game though

on special oc

casions they
may adopt an

almost serious
ly acceptable-

countenance.

When the (2)

a) sea's become

as smooth as

a lake smooth
es over as

well at time
s ruffled con

b) templation

s leaving be

hind but a
spaciously

conceived time–
release.

Are the wave (3)

a) s or the self-

withholding

quietude
s that con

tinue to

b) assemble my

poetic re
flection

s ashore It'
s become hard

to distin

c) guish the diff

erences while
they must some

how realise
that themsel

ves.

If it's (2)

a) one of those

soft-down-

poems will
soon discover

its own route
s levelling

b) one's own

thought

s to a spec
ially word-re

fined sensi
bility.

Leafless si

lences those
speechless

symptoms of
winter's bare-

faced lost-re
membrance

s.

That straw (3)

   a) berry bass I

   hooked decade

   s ago in Lake
   Champlain

   b) with its al

   most taste

   ful look re
   sembling it's

   berried name-
   sake left such

   c) a lasting im

   pression as

   it slid-off
   my own hook

   ed-down-pre
   sence.

When can (3)

> *a) words however*
>
> over-used mis-
>
> used be res
> cued from

> *b) their adoles*
>
> cent habitat
>
> "Thrilled" for
> example in a
>
> purely physi
> cal-sense "Awe

> *c) some" and "fabu*
>
> lous" remain
>
> at least
> for me out–
>
> of-reach a
> helpless cause.

Finely express (2)

a) *ive tropical*

leaves me trans

parently ex
posed to what

remains just

b) *listening to*

the wave's

repetitive
tide-reawak

ening
s.

If the Turk *(4)*

a) s would attack

again what

they once
possessed

b) for centurie

s diverting

as semi-dict
ator from

internal pro

c) blems who

would help
defend this

also NATO tiny-
peopled-island

d) with no more

inhabitant

s than all of
Munich's self-

reclaiming
citizen

s.

Has that well (2)

a) *ness-feeling*

without ache

s and pain
s and organ

ic disturban
ces become

b) *what most a*

ging person

s would glad
ly daily con

ceive as
life–itself.

Other direct *(3)*

a) ioned He some

what older

swam just as
far as he

possibly

b) could out-to-

sea looking
more like a

young "vacat
ion date"

swam other

c) wise direct

ioned way-
out along the

solo thing-
reach of a

shore-line.

He a middle- *(3)*

a) aged loner

along with a
most confident

ial book

b) paged with an

almost undue
reverence

eyed the late
afternoon'

c) s incoming

waves with

that off-shor
ed kind of

distancing-
denial.

Sea-timed *(3)*

    a) stone-collect

    ors (you can

    even sense
    them from a

    b) distance)

    their open–

    eyed feet-em
    bracing self–

    reassuring

    c) slow-timed

    aesthetical
    ly indulging

    momentary
    aha–pause

    s.

Does the *(2)*

    a) weaver weave

    his own self–

    reflective
    thought

    s into the

    b) fabric of

    that cloth'
    s pre–deter

    mining de
    sign

    s.

Why do (2)

a) these Cypri

otic hills

keep climb
ing through

my own self–

b) vacanting

thought
s when they'

ve become im
movably land

scaped.

She remain (3)

a) ed that sugar-

and–cream–

type with a
hardened

b) will pressing

her daily keep-

down–below re
ligiously as

piring yet as

c) wordly as if

she'd just
earned her

first time-
holding doll

ar.

Early even

ing shadow
s though

weightless
leave the

impression
of a darken

ing self-en
compassing

metaphysi
cal-force.

He dream

ed the sea
out beyond

the expanse
of his own

rhymed-imag
ining

s.

Usually (3)

a) *the early*

morning land

scaping's
enough to

b) *set-off my*

multi-phased

poetic respon
se If not

earlier poem
s may help

c) *me writing-*

through to

a receptive
sense–encom

passing dia
logue.

For some (3)

>>> *a) especially*

>>> T. V. and Holly

>>> wood film-wat
>>> chers it

>>> *b) may not seem*

>>> implausible

>>> but thorough
>>> ly-imaginable

>>> for Aphrodite

>>> *c) to emerge fully-*

>>> beautified
>>> from the puri

>>> fying-depth
>>> s of the Ae

>>> gean Sea.

It remain (3)

a) s hard to

deny that the

stronger the
deeper love

b) takes-hold

of one's en

tire-being
possessive

ly-sourced

c) even to the

depths of un
founded Othell

ian-jealou
sy.

What kind of (3)

a) an unusual

semi-tropical

tree was that
which we just

b) passed with

its bark peel

ing-off as a
snake shedd

ing its skin
a necessary

c) cure perhaps

for person

s as Trump
too daily

self-orient
ed.

This island' *(2)*

> *a) s so flourish*

ing even with

unsuspect
ing flowering

s that it

> *b) seems to have*

been specially
favored by a

daily-aspir
ing inevit

able-sun.

Americana (7)

   a) Broadway

shows and

musicals the
American mean

   b) s of activat

ing tough–

minded busin
ess men and

women to the

   c) softer side

of life's sen
sual pleasur

ings and un
fortunately

   d) our Jewish-

own composer

s Rodgers
Gerschwin

and Bernstein

e) accomodating

to the lower-
levelled Ameri

can's no qual
ity comparison

f) for our German

and Austrian

Jewish Mendels
sohn and even

Mahler but

g) most especially

those quality
writers as

Kafka Heine
Celan and …

There are (9)

a) *those especial*

creative art

ists as Shakes
peare and Haydn

b) *intuned in a*

very special

way to the
audience

they helped

c) *create*

whereas Fontane
perhaps Germany'

s greatest
novelist wrote

d) for a special

class the Junker

s such as Bis
marck who didn'

t read his

e) books had to

become satis
fied much to

his own sur
prise with a

f) largely Jew

ish audience

foreign to
his own rai

son d'être

g) Whom do we

really write-
for our own

aesthetic-
pleasure an

h) audience that'

s yet to be

come fully-
cultivated

a distant God

i) (poetas) or

is it the poem
that writes-us-

through its
own-sensi

bility.

Even at 7:30

the sun's ris
en to a pre-

establish
ed–height

assuming its
own voiced-

growth even
now its flour

ishing time-
length.

Tradition (3)

a) alists How far

down an early

Byzantine
church has

b) sunk into

its depthed-

stature's a
secondary

means of de

c) riving its

time-length
ening spirit

ual–effect
iveness.

Are most cat' (2)

a) s inordinate

need for clean

liness (and
this hotel's

swarming with
them) a Lady

b) Macbeth type

of reaction

to killing–
off another

too-late-wing
èd bird-or–

two.

It wasn't (3)

a) easy for Mary

to bring-up

a perfect per
son realising

b) almost daily

how imperfect

even she had
remained That

's one of the

c) main reasons

Jesus was hated

and then kill
ed by his

very imperfect–
opponent

s.

Low-level

scrubs ground–
based escort

ing the rock
ed surfacing

a landscape
dried–down

to its essen
tial inhab

iting life-
source.   ·

"The Legend" (4)

a) *The 2nd or*

even 3rd rate

MacDonald's
hamburger

b) *s now referr*

ed too almost

with a certain
reverence as

"The Legend"

c) *perhaps of Rip*

van Winkle's
sleeping-off

the gastron
omic effect

d) *s of such a*

tasteless

hardly–identi
fiable bur

ger.

The ever- *(4)*

a) present sun

rules this is

land with a
brightness

b) that defies

our earth–

bound dark
nesses (one be

gins to under
stand here

c) why ancient

peoples wor

shipped such
an empowering

sun) for
it even calls

d) the indwell

ing flower

s to its
daily color–

distribut
ing voice.

This will *(4)*

a) long-be-remem

bered as The

Corona Year
2020 spread

b) ing its at

times deadly

invisible
virus through

the veins and

c) heart-beat

of our self–
certaining

It's ours for

d) the ruling o

ver life love

and a God
less–human

ity.

Even though *(3)*

a) I'm supposedly
90% green
blind I can
still appre

b) ciate the
life-reclaim
ing landscap
ing of this
color's refresh

c) ing innovat
ive finely dis
tributing
growth-find
s.

Those rand (2)

a) om ships out

at sea seem

to be calling
my word-re

claiming dis
tances phrased

b) through the

poetic-wave

s of a time
lessly recurr

ing tidal-
source.

Critics who (3)

a) tend to reclaim

these self-a

vailing poem
s of mine

b) for their own

pre-determin

ing scholar
ly schemes

will learn in
time that such

c) elusive poetry

will alway

s determine
its own self-

desiring
course.

Our two *(6)*

> *a) presidential*
>
> candidate
>
> s 2020 repre
> sent a rather

> *b) lower-level*
>
> contrast of
>
> two vastly
> differing
>
> personality–

> *c) types The one*
>
> always Trump
> First never re
>
> treating alway
> s attacking

d) never conced

ing his numer

ous oft damag
ing mistake

s The other

e) of somewhat

lesser intell
igence usually

trying to har
monise person

al and politi

f) cal differen

ces though at
the oncoming

age of a
slightly de

mense-impress
ion.

One must be (4)

a) prepared to

realise sub

tle differen
ces while

b) distinguish

ing the not-

so-otherwise-
routes of

Byzantine

c) art It's per

haps the
similar

prayer–invok
ing-spirit

d) uality that

unites centur

ies of a not-
so-innovat

ive religious
art.

We paint *(5)*

a) we write

we compose

what we are
for some as

b) Bach Shakes

peare Rembran

dt and Haydn
the world of

vastly en

c) during dimen

sions For some
as Ruisdael

and Webern
a very sin

d) gular but lim

ited thematic

display For
still other

s as Carissimi

e) and Matthew

Arnold but a
one-work of

lasting-
greatness.

Fall in (3)

a) Cyprus still

a leaf-fall

ing time be
cause of or

b) even despite

the hot summ

er weather
's-span Oct

ober here's
a time of

c) seasonal al

ways inter

changeable
expressive

ness.

The older (3)

a) they get the

brighter

more decorat
ive their

b) dresses blou

ses and skirt

s become Why
this reawaken

ing of earl
ier I may

c) still feel

that way at

odd-moment
s yet ever–

slightly so.

The sea' (3)

a) s become but

softly-voiced

this morning
The waves

b) lessened to

their almost

timeless pre
sence Even the

surrounding

c) hills more

like spectat

ors of what'
s still re

mains life-e
merging.

When indoor

s become as
well outdoor

s as with De
Hooch's so-

called interior-
scenes Space

takes-on a
uniform self-

encompass
ing silence.

The who is (3)

a) What if Rosemar

ie usually

thinks the
best of new

b) ly-arrived-per

sons took him

for an under
world law-es

caping German
whereas I

c) taken by his

aesthetical

ly-involving
discoverie

s hoping for
more person

al-contact.

It had be (3)

a) *come more*

like that

float–me–a
sail kind of

b) *sea-calling*

weather

but the lack
of a steady

hold of those
sand–shift

c) *ings phrased*

him to his

usual chair–
espying look–

out post.

I speak too (3)

> *a) loudly for her*

> provoking

> unease while
> She speak

> s too quiet

> *b) ly for my*

> 60% hearing
> with one aid

> not function
> ing for me

> *c) to understand*

> What we're

> saying if at
> best a non-

> receptive
> together

> ness.

The prevail (3)

a) *ing weather'*

s become so

continuous
ly blue as

b) *if time's re*

mained unable

to think-out
an otherwise-

coloring

c) *as persons*

routined
to a daily

intermin
able-task.

If life's (2)

  a) nothing but a

  dream as Calder

  on and Haydn
  would assure

  us When does

  b) it wake-up

  to an unknown
  world of a

  darkly treas
  ured–respon

  se.

Mooned (2)

a) The nearby

sea keeps dis

covering the
rhythmic

flow of my

b) own verse

daily awaken
ed through

its tidal–
indwelling

source.

He towering (2)

    a) over all the

    other hotel

    guests She
    presumably

    his wife

    b) petite half-

    sized only
    to the height

    of his Hercu
    lean shoulder-

    length.

I've never (3)

    a) thought of

    myself as a

    lady's man
    as Uncle Phil

    b) statured to

    many woman'

    s more than
    dreamed-to

    getherness
    But many seem

    c) to have dis

    covered my

    "Adonis-like"
    darkly-browned-

    feature
    s.

Extreme (2)

a) *imperialist*

ic national

ists as Napol
ean and Hitler

have bloodied
their nation

b) *permanently*

down to but

a paled-imitat
ion of a once-

timed great
ness.

Our turtler *(3)*

a) *s are miss*

ing this year

even though
their turtle

b) *friends may*

well be miss

ing their out–
spreading

following–

c) *through per*

spective

d watering
time–phase

s.

These sunny (4)

a) cloudless

Cyprian Oct

ober days
no longer

b) seem certain

ly identifia

ble (perhaps
s only through

my daily poeti

c) cally compos

ed diary) They
still seem in

tent as much
Byzantine

d) art on most

ly copying their

once-tim
ed significant

ly adept-prede
cessor

s.

Paradise (3)

> *a) Garden for Savas*
>
> and Carola
>
> If paradise
> means living

> *b) through one'*
>
> s own garden
>
> ed–fruits
> then pick–
>
> them–as–you–
> please guavas

> *c) kingly pome*
>
> granats and
>
> their accom
> paning royal–
>
> entourage.

False or (2)

a) fake news

a subtle BBC

variant pre
senting Trump'

s rough and
ready renegade–

b) type whereas

Biden's support

ers young lib
eral and ex

pressively
fair-minded.

Curtain (2)

a) s have become

in Cyprus more

like women's
self-chosen

dresses at
once charact

b) er-express

ing a privacy

of formly
touched–through

protective–
length

s.

My mother *(4)*

a) claimed that

churches look

ed all-the–
same to her

b) But I'm most

certain that

newly conceiv
ed synagogue

s remained

c) for her not

only variable
but interest

ing as well
We all tend

d) to see and

realise best

what's closer
to our own i

denity-claim
s.

Early morn (3)

a) ing swimmer

s refresh

ing the day
through their

b) own bodily de

signs Even

the sea help
ed smooth-o

ver whatever
remained of

c) the night'

s pre-estab

lishing
dreamed-dark

nesses.

I've never (3)

a) seen a cat

spotted more

like a leo
pard should

b) be inhabit

ing the local

zoo while
here its jung

led instinct
s just wait

c) ing cat-like

for an aggress

ive self-ex
pressive

ness.

Everything' (2)

> *a) s blossoming*

> here perhap

> s of their   `

> own selective

> colorings
> or has that

> *b) been pre-deter*

> mined as a

> bouquet of
> freshly-cho

> sen eye-appeal
> ings.

Stern-look *(3)*

a) ing middle-
aged German
women have
provided per
haps a con

b) tinuity of
Adenauer'
s "It's
never been
so serious"
Yet this one

c) say in her
mid or late
30s evokes an
almost chill
ing-expectan
cy.

Answering John (5)

a) *A. Crowe Despite*

the usual intro

duction there'
s little to

b) *be found even*

in the example

s he himself
has chosen of

the pastoral–

c) *ideal in the*

great Spanish
Rennaissance

poet Garcilaso'
s tensioned

d) *verse between*

an unrequited

love Catullus–
like and death'

s all–consum

e) ing call What'
s left then
for personal

idyllic soul–
satisfaction

s.

Mooned? (3)

a) Is this sea

sourced with

a temperament
of its own

b) acting-out

its at time

s disturbing
emotional-re

straints or is

c) it only being

mooned by dis
tant tidal-a

wakening
s.

Garcilaso' (2)

a) *s most spec*

ial way of

surprising
twists and

turns his
listener

b) *into the pass*

ion of a

poet's self-
reflecting

love-pain
s.

The waves (3)

a) are breaking

high this

afternoon'
s no mean

b) s of securing

a lasting

foot-hold
Fun for the

children

c) 's momentar

ily breaking-
free from

their parent
al-restraint

s.

Walking-the- *(3)*

a) beach with no

particular

purpose in–
mind except

b) perhaps the

occasional

unusual de
signed–stone

but while

c) poetically

rhymed to the
sea's bluster

ing–excitabil
ity.

First scanty (2)

a) *clouds blown-*

through with

a let's-hurry-
to-get-there

attitude as

b) *if there's*

continual
ly remain

ing what's
still further-

on.

On and off (8)

   a) Luise Glück

   and the Nobel

   Prize for
   literature

   b) 's remained

   an on-and-off

   -kind-of-thing
   Tolstoi the

   greatest of

   c) novelists

   and Kafka the
   most original

   writer of the
   20th century

   d) were passed-

   by many 2nd rate

   writers as
   Bob Dylan

   who's not e

e) ven that

have been a
warded Luise

Glück's a
good and able

f) poetess more

traditional

while lack
ing real origin

g) ality-distinct

ions both in
her use of

language
and the depth

s of her in

h) sights Next to

the peace-prize
the literary

one remains an
on-and-off

kind-of-thing.

Early morn (3)

a) *ing's sleepful*

ness a silence

pervading the
very life–

b) *sense of this*

unawaken

ed landscap
ing the sun'

s heralded–

c) *call over the*

sea's carrier
s of wave-im

pulsing re
newal life–

source.

Why these (3)

a) self-suffi

cient dark-

phases that
would reclaim

our entire

b) life-span

for their own
self-purpos

ings The devil
and the deep

could be call

c) ed and I c

ven poem-an
nulled from

life's beauti
fying-express

iveness.

Tiny flie (2)

a) s insisting

their disturb

ing presence
My father

once remarked

b) "little per

sons need to
feel big when

ever the oppor
tunity arise

s".

"Inextinguishable" (7)

a) Is the form

of each day
the coloring

of its hand–
selective

b) flowers and

the inbreed

ing of the
sea's necess

ary tidal–

d) pulse Are

creations e
ven more than

a daily re

d) newal of life'

s persisting
inextinguish

able–presen
ce Nielsen'

e) s 3 great sym

phonies the

3rd 4th and
5th facing up

to man's in
evitable ever–

f) repetitive

self–destruct

iveness with
the creative

answer of man'

g) s equally renewa

ble "inexting
uishable"

search–for–
meaning.

How often *(4)*

a) has the under

standing of

a most per
sonal problem

b) become a mean

s not for

change but
for I know

the impending

c) length and

depth of its
repetitive

effects much

d) like primitive

man painting-
out its game-

providing hun
ter's.

If love' (2)

a) s the essence

of life's

meaning not a
willful act

but a pre-
given gift one

b) cannot aspire

to its bene

fits but only
wait in a

somehow fully
prepared–re

ceptivity.

If what (2)

a) *seems to be*

true one day

but most like
ly not so

the next Have
I changed or

b) *has the elus*

ive answer

ing escaped
from a "time

less" pre-giv
en truth.

Why did *(5)*

a) that distant

relative law

yer-of-a-per
son wait at

b) family funct

ions especial

ly for me with
his usual "un

answerable
question" Was

c) he simply show

ing-off his

not-knowing
Socratic-wis

dom Why the

d) son of (in fin

ancial terms)
more success

ful lawyer Or
the otherwise

me a Christian

e) with a set of

perhaps reveal
ing answers

to his other
wise unanswer

able
s.

Annulled? *(4)*

a) He listened

as hard as

he could to
those unhear

b) able hearing-

aid words

Had they
sought refuge

from his poet

c) ic-grasp or

had they be
come annulled

as unrealise
able word–

d) finds but try

as hard as

he could
heard noth

ing.

When the (2)

a) heat's intensi

fying beyond

the scope of
my poetic con

centration
I must flee

b) as the Daphne-

of–other–

causes into
a newly tree–

aspiring other
wise–lifeful

ness.

Steven Forster (2)

a) *our minor Schu*

bert keeps sing

ing-to-mind
not as those

lower classed
childhood song

b) *s but touch*

ing the accord

s of a depth
ed-feeling

still relevant
ly time-tell

ing.

The sea' (3)

a) s quieted-down

once again as

if reconsider
ing its after

b) noon excita

bility It'

s become like
my still empt

ied writing-pad

c) still waiting

to become

thoroughly
written–

through wave–
like.

Flag waving *(4)*

a) was never our

family's sort-

of-thing I
felt deeply em

b) barassed while

pledging alle

giance to a
flag especial

ly after that
fake-news

c) from our vic

tory in Iwo

Jima-flag held
by soldier

s soon to be
declared dead

d) nevertheless

that fake-

news used es
pecially on

the Iwo Jima
victory-stamp

s.

Most diffi (4)

a) cult for pat

riotic Ameri

can Jews to
realise that

b) Roosevelt our

hero knew of

Auschwitz
and the other

camps but did

c) nothing to

prevent the

mass–killing
s As the bible

repeatedly

d) emphasized

Don't trust
other power

s only The Lord
our God.

Sparrows (4)

a) just arrived

Could you be

lieve their
addition

b) to those "en

dangered spec

ies" hopping a
bout their

food–surviv

c) ing-hunger-

routes steal
ing – if

they can get
away with it

d) the crumbs

of their fell

ow–creature
s shortly-

held appetiz
ers.

Friday's (2)

> *a) the black cat'*

s specially-

designed day
recalling some

long-since-
forgotten evil

> *b) -doings perhap*

s witched with

the broom-
stick's long—

reaching ab
ductive success—

route.

Do Bikini *(3)*

a) ladies espec

ially prefer

the feel of
the wind and

b) waves refresh

ing their

self-display
ing half-nak

edness or
those men's

c) eyes surfac

ing the full

extent of
their enti

cing expos
ures.

Why those (3)

a) *4 so central*

saints mystic

s and poets
of the Span

b) *ish Rennais*

sance of Jew

ish descent
all tested by

the Inquisit

c) *ion of their*

Jewish blood
ran dry (1492)

shortly there
after.

Weimar on (4)

a) *the streets of*

America Armed

gangs half–an
archaic half–

b) *ideological*

facing–each–o

ther with the
more or less

tacit support

c) *of the two-*

partied leader
ship The guilt

is shared not

d) *one-sided as*

both sides
would like

to envision–
it.

The spirit (5)

a) ual love of

the Spanish

Rennaissan
ce often

b) poets of Jew

ish descent

transcend
ing as with

Donne and Her
bert the "lower–

c) levelled earthy

sensual–sort"

And yet despite
my unreling

uishable faith

d) I'd still pre

fer what's
nearer to my

earth–bound
here and

now and momen

e) tarily nowhere'

s else but not so
intent as Lope'

s increasing
ly sensual–

lust.

Rather ugly *(3)*

a) Bikini ladies

in their 70s

posing as
photo–model

b) s Whom are

they trying

to convince
except them

selves We all

c) inhabit more

or less a
goodly port

ion of wish
ful-thinking.

There have (3)

> *a) been several*
>
> animal-fable
>
> moralists as
> the Greek slave

> *b) Aesop in var*
>
> ied language
>
> s as French
> Russian and
>
> English Here
> perhaps lies

> *c) the unifying*
>
> psychology
>
> of man's class
> and timeless
>
> essential–
> being.

What should- *(2)*

a) be-said and

what you-want-

to-say often
remains in

conflict with
each-other

b) Although for

those temper

amentally-
sourced the

solution
remains quick-

at-hand.

Is it (3)

> a) those new

ly-sensed

flowers that
redefine my

> b) half color-

blind wheres

and where
fores of a

garden pleas

> c) ured with

daily-sensed
unexpected

beautifying-
encounter

s.

When I (3)

a) *only hear 60%*

with one of

my hearing
aids not funct

b) *uning and with*

that unquiet

in the hotel'
s dining room

I feel as

c) *if cast-off*

to a non-com
munitive

if semi-perman
ent silenc

ing.

He's the (2)

a) *easily-excit*

able-type

but as straw
fires just as

easily burn

b) *ed-out their*

much less than
lasting inflam

ed emotional
ly ignited–

purposings.

It's diffi (5)

a) *cult not to*

admire New York

but equally
difficult

b) *for some to*

take it person

ally to heart
I felt that

way about the

c) city where this

poet was born
Only once when

it lay under
the Great Blizz

d) ard of '47

and all of

its business
es became still

ed and distan

c) ces and remote

silences be
gan to speak

in a language
of their own.

What one *(3)*

a) will remember

of Cyprus

months from
now the color

b) ful flowering

s and the

sea birthed
from a self–

perpetuating

c) sun and the

eternal moon
's tidal lyri

cal time-
grasp.

One should *(4)*

a) have realised

his chosen

profession
from the jagg

b) ed contour

s of his self–

proclaiming
head-set in

a mountain
guide steep–

c) ed in those

useable trail

s that the
mountain

s themselv
es had left

d) providing

for discover

ers time-with
holding a

wareness
es.

Shakespear (4)

a) *ean The scen*

ery's now

in the midst
of its usual

b) *generation-*

change while

we in our
80s aspire a

holding-on

c) *as long as*

we can as
my 104-year-

old-mother

d) *to what's be*

ing put-aside
for a last

(ing) forget
fullness.

Unforget (3)

a) able as the

past here in
Germany still

b) hovering as

birds of prey

over a land
buried as deep

ly as possible

c) in its once-

upon-a-time
still haunt

ing-relevan
ces.

Should one *(3)*

a) best under

stand Cyprus

as America
from its on

b) going outside

influence

s or as Freder
ick Jackson

Turner for A

c) merica's contin

uity of its
indigenous

prioritie
s.

Up today (3)

a) to those con

cealed from

the Turks
mountain

ed church
es who slash

b) ed a way if

possible the

New Testament
frescos while

reserving
those of the

c) Old for

their own

historical–
theological–

relevance.

One must (3)

a) *"have a mind"*

for poetry

as Borges and
T. S. Eliot

b) *to distin*

guish between

the necessary
and the ex

traneous But

c) *too much of*

such can hin
der the indig

enous poetic–
flow.

Does history

shape us or
we it or is

history it
self an on

going time-ex
tending dia

logue between
ever-change

able person
and place.

One can't (4)

a) measure the

depth of a

believer'
s faith

b) through the

number and

quality of
his or her

good work

c) s But with

out them
such a so-

called "faith"
would remain

d) fruitless

ly abstract

as a leaf
less winter

ed-tree.

Those barren (3)

a) *October hill*

s reaching

empty-handed
for the once

b) *flourish*

ing cultur

al-height
s leaving

only in spring
time the decor

c) *ative-flower*

ings at the

grave of a
once-timed

greatness.

Merkel o (2)

a) *pened the door*

wide for the

Arab–Moslem
migrants

Now she's
time-retell

b) *ing the anti-*

semetic still

open–wound
s of Germany'

s Jew–blood
ed phantom–

ed past.

Two-timed (3)

a) These mount

ainous vast

ly under
ground root

b) ed (routed)

trees spread

ing-out im
portant infor

mation while

c) holding-back

the threaten
ing rocks from

their imman
ent slide-ap

parencie
s.

The Annun (4)

a) ciation at

Pedouslas

1494 with that
angel seeming

ly mid-air

b) while equal

ly neverthe
less aware of

his most-im
portant messa

c) ging

s St. George

there fully-
armed decorat

ively-horsed

d) but with a

most Christ
ian humbly

sourced-ex
pressive

ness.

Arthur Rackham-

like fantastic
tree-distort

ed configur
ations a

witchery
of out-reach

ing poss
essive

ness.

Terracing

the landscape
and the hou

ses leaves
the lasting

impression
of a thrif

ty but class-
oriented

society.

The aband

oned hills of
Cyprus remain

not only
steadfast

ly worthy
while in Oct

ober's late
afternoon

sun-proof
as-well.

The Troodoos *(4)*

a) mountain'

s car-curv

ing left them
passengered

to those habit
ual-unbalanc

b) ing strange

ly roofed

churches' den
ial of the a

lien Moslem–
Earth.

c) At such time

s one would

have prefer
ed being bird

d) ed straight-

lined sky-

bound to our
coveted-des

tination.

Savas our (3)

　　a) friendly taxi-

　　driver remind

　　ing us year-
　　for-year of

　　b) his enormous

　　Händelian-

　　proportion
　　ed appetite

　　and the ful

　　c) ness of his

　　learned e
　　qually expan

　　sive know-
　　how.

No one (5)

a) can be guaran

teed which of

the 10 U. N.
's sanctif

b) ied churches

will be open

ed always o
therwise on

Saturday It'

c) s a hit-and-

miss kind-of-
thing often

after an in
tricate trail

d) of repetitious

curve-invok

ing expectat
ions of a

e) church-with

holding and o

pen-door re
sponse.

Rosemarie (5)

a) *at 82 our*

cultural-

guide still re
taining her

b) *innocent*

little-girl

Gretchen-
like appeal

Though there'

c) *s a self-cer*

tainty about
her lost father

only child
ness After al

d) *most 60 year*

s of an un

usual self-
fulfilling

marriage we'
ve become as

e) interdepend

ent as Mozart

and Haydn Wein
berg and Shosta

kovich.

The spider' (2)

a) s net-wise

aesthetic–

appeal some
how intricate

ly involved

b) in death'

s increasing
ly visible

timely–claim
s.

The sea (3)

a) however famil

iar it's be

come through
our repetit

ive long–

b) range view

still daily
awakens a

sense of
I'm still

there new

c) ly accompan

ing your o
therwise

time-shift
ing presen

ce.

Blue (2)

a) Bellini-blue
Rosemarie
especial
ly in light–
blue This

b) daily blue
sky's express
ing a heaven
ly-sourced
blue-beginn
ings.

When these (4)

a) semi-tropical

roses start

losing their
petals we

b) somehow

feel a sense–

of–loss too
similar to

aggressive

c) Lesbic women

taking the
most beauti

fying young

d) ladies a

way from
our self-de

signing in
tention

s.

Letter-writ (3)

a) ing for the

very-few re

mains these
days like com

b) posing a work

-of-art but

for a spec
ial recipient

Perhaps even

c) as with Mendels

sohn with
lasting person

al-impress
ions.

Because of (2)

    a) this intri

cately-compos

ed cloud-cele
bration

s but only
momentarily

    b) with a heaven

ly-expressive

ness will soon
move-on but

then most cer
tainly other

wise-phased.

These soft (2)

a) ly-situated

cumulous

clouds rest
ing their

supremely

b) self-satisfy

ing quietude
s as those re

nowned cloud-
sitting-on

angel
s.

Some of (3)

a) *these narrow-*

streeted

medieval
towns as in

b) *Apulia leave-*

the-impress

ion of a
world–left–

behind that
still contin

c) *ues shadow*

ing us with

its darkly-
secluded phan

tomed-presen
ce.

"They're just (2)

a) Jews" she said

as if Jesus

Mary Peter and
Paul weren't

also "just
Jews" or more

b) probably she

meant rather

highly-sour
ced "They're

the ones who
killed-their-

own-king".

Waiting for (3)

> *a) that five-en*

tombed tower

ed medieval
church to be

> *b) opened for a*

tradition

al Orthodox
wedding I

felt myself
almost centur

> *c) ies old for*

its time–ex

tending re
ceptive beau

ties.

One dead (2)

a) tree with its

bare dangling

speechless-
branches on

a flourish
ing hill–

b) side of leaf

ed purposing

Perhaps as a
warning who–

will-be-the-
next.

An even- *(2)*

    a) sounding

    poem's like

    a well–groom
    ed man who

    continue
    s to make a

    b) self-inhabit

    ing though

    steadily per
    sonally con

    trolled–im
    pression.

He built his (4)

a) bare-headed

ugliness in

to a muscular
ly-tensed-ap

b) petite for

his favorite

tomato soup
3 times serv

ed hat still

c) on in a creat

ured inhalat
ing way yet in

conversation

d) he seemed at

least humane
ly even per

sonally-nor
mal.

Cyprus so (4)

a) near to Israel

and untouched

by Nazi anti-
semetic barbar

b) ism never re

linguishing

(even under Turk
ish rule) its

ground-based

c) deeply relig

ious-tradition
s But who will

defend it if
once again

d) attacked by

its NATO Turk

ish too-close
ly inhabiting-

neighbor
s.

"Handwrit (4)

    a) ings on the

    wall" America

    perhaps too
    (two) heavily–

    b) armed-camp

    s divided at

    the very-root
    s of its his

    torical social

    c) religious and

    even economic
    -political

    tradition
    (never a real

    d) melting-pot)

    to become not

    only in name
    a singular

    ly united nat
    ion?

Our taxi *(6)*

a) driver with

whom we've

developed
more than

b) just a sight-

seeing relation

suffering from
an acute Adler

ian inferior

c) ity complex

"I'm just a
taxi-driver

no one take
s me serious

d) ly as with

lawyers for ex

ample" I answer
ed "This island

lives from tour

e) ism Without

taxis and taxi-
drivers it could

n't flour
ish and who

f) needs lawyer

s anyway

"words of wis
dom" from a

lawyer-bred
family.

Perhaps *(5)*

a) it's social

backward

ness or a
deeply root

b) ed (routed)

Judaic–Christ

ian tradit
ion but our

three-time

c) s motherly

hostess in
cluded her

own aging mo
ther in their

d) most family-

conscious

ness not only
included but

e) actually

seen as a con

tinual–source
of timely–wis

dom.

It took (4)

a) more than a

convention

al puppy-wis
dom for their

b) home-groom

ed dog to ac

cept that
this stranger

(me) could

c) imitate a

young dog's

bark so
successful

ly that it

d) seemed to

question
ably accept

him as one-
of-their-

own.

"He (Savas) (4)

    a) has seen and

    visited more
    of the histori

    ic churches

    b) on this island

    than even the
    its most pious

    inhabitant
    s" That as

    c) my historic

    al–minister

    ial means of
    increasing

    d) his pious and

    attractive

    wife's inner
    most priori

    ties.

Few tourist *(3)*

a) s here and

anywhere

's else have
establish

ed such a per

b) sonal relat

ion with its
still activat

ing inhabit
ants That'

c) s tourism on a

deeper and

more personal-
historical

ground-right
s basis.

The continu (3)

a) ous so-called

manly war-addic
ted hardly

seems worthy
of his high–

b) levelled

creation

al rights
that Haydn's

great biblical
ly-based Creat

c) ion sounds to

day with the

creation of
man almost

self-ironi
cal.

This still (3)

a) morning's

fully power

ful–Cypriot
ic–autumnal–

b) sun continue

s to re–estab

lish its creat
ional–claim

s as a daily–

c) embodying

source of
light life and

whatever's
beautifying

ly–coloring.

Tourism (4)

a) People should

remain more

important
than even his

b) torical place

s Depthed-tour

ism's on a
personal

basis not

c) only realis

ing the cultur
al–historical

past's should
remain more im

d) portant than

those daily

umbrella–
heightened

beach–claim
s.

That walled (3)

    a) in walled-out

    monastery

    to provide
    both protect

    b) ion from the

    outside as

    well as the
    insides seclu

    sion for its

    c) religious

    ly-depthed

    godly-dedicat
    ed monk

    s.

Fewer and few (4)

a) er tourists

now almost mid–
October when
the weather

b) and the wa

ter's so com

pletely tour
ist–accomodat

ing and Corona'

d) s almost been

totally held–
off from this

paradisical

d) island as

most all

seen or invis
ible invader

s.

When Europe' (3)

a) s denying the

suitability

of crosses in
public place

b) s It's also

denying its

religious
and histori

cal heritage

c) It won't take

long for o
thers to fill

that identity-
gap.

That late-vin (3)

a) tage Shakes

peare's inter

est in seclud
ed peaceful

b) and almost

magically

inhabited
islands would

Cyprus today
satisfy

c) much of The

Great Bard'
s ahistori

cal post-dra
matic–claim

s.

Some of (2)

a) the beach

stones have

become so in
tricately

written–
through that

b) one might

wonder if

handwriting
hadn't been

so–origin
ed.

The water' (2)

a) s roughing-

up again This

sea's change
able moods

seem so char
acterist

b) ic of certain-

kinds-of-hu

man-behavior
that it's be

come almost
personalis

ed for me.

Open-borders *(3)*

a) If open-

borders had
become a most

intimate

b) trade-mark

of a United
Europe then

Corona's un
done such a

c) Europe leav

ing it once

again to it's
most-vital

national-in
terest

s.

We've now (4)

    a) 3 lifeguard

s for at

most 15 per
sons beached

    b) here for plea

sure One of

them's poised
to pull Rose

marie out of

    c) the gravel-

shifting wa
ters Such per

sonal service

    d) almost unique

in tourist
sea-side re

sort
s.

Beach-comb (3)

a) ers a once

quite popular

English title
to be reacti

vated as Cor

b) ona world-wide

combings for
shells if they'

re any left
to be found

on as Rosemar

c) ie for stone

s insignaed
with the in

dwelling rhy
thmic life-of–

the–sea.

Savas' cat (4)

a) s trophaed him

though modest

ly presented
at the door

b) step's rat'

s heads dead

mice and even
a poisoned

snake or two
His thorough

c) ly-fruited para

dise-garden

animalled
too with those

classically
oriented cat

d) s sanction

ed for the

necessary
garden clean

ing-up opera
tion

s.

This newly *(3)*

a) inaugurated

wind-wave dia

logue has
brought with

b) it an appro

priate scenery-

change cloud-
skied for the

most necess
ary oncoming

c) approval or

more like a

heavenly-spon
sored fash

ion-show.

Life must (3)

a) go on monied

future-perspec

tives even if
Corona's been

b) scheduled

in that same

balance-sheet
It's like

finishing-

c) up a job

that's not
yours to be

done thorough
ly-finalis

ed.

The tourist (4)

a) s mainly Engl

ish Russian

Israelis used
to October

b) this island

with their

mostly lower-
level aims

But now they'
re all high-

c) listed on Cor

ona's creative

byways Only the
Germans left

d) to language

this island

anew with beer
and celebrat

ing mood
s.

Some hear *(7)*

a) poems to hear

what they
like-to-hear

b) Others would

prefer a new

frame-of-re
ference even

quite differ

c) ent from their

own The poet
himself most

ly listen
ing to what

d) the poem's

telling him

on its own
aesthetic

merits Beau

e) ty continue

s to respond
to its own

indigenous-
qualitie

f) s when word

s space-out

their necess
ary breathing-

scope and when
ideas become

g) newly clothed

in otherwise-

considered
forms and color

ings.

Such a vast (3)

a) *assemblage of*

individual

ly-rowed early
morning Cyprio

b) *tic clouds*

rarely to be

seen and other
wise out-of-

bounds of the
new Corona

c) *rules as to*

the allowed

number for
such-presenta

tion
s.

That last- (6)

a) day-feeling
of what used
to become an
impending

b) sense-of-loss
but now at
our advanced
age more as
if time had

c) fully complet
ed our–justi
fied claims
for rest for
swims (Rose

d) marie) for

cultural sight

s even repeat
ed ones of

Christian

e) and aestheti

cally more than
for personal

appreciation
this October

f) book of poem

s from Cyprus

being written
down to its

lasting
breath.

Cyprus has be *(3)*

a) come our own

post-Shakes

pearean para
disic October–

b) island with

out it our

mapped-out
October-life

would become

c) personally

cultural
ly and poeti

cally lost a
cross the

seas.

Rarely if e (4)

a) *ver have we*

establish

ed a deeper
personal con

b) *tact with o*

ther tourist

s not because
we (or better-

put) I haven'
t often tried

c) *but a life-*

of-two seem

s actually
more-than-e

nough to dia
logue the var

d) *ied beautie*

s of such a

paradisic is
land as our

Cyprus.

Something (4)

a) *missing here*

not only the

Corona stay-
at-homes or

b) *persons-non-*

grata tourist

s Yes they'
re still fish

swimming
these most

c) *out fished*

Mediterranean

waters but
despite a

still–active
bird life no

d) *wild-life dead*

or alive to

accompany
us through

our October-
pilgrammage.

Have Aron *(4)*

a) and Alena been

called to re

place us when
the time come

b) s but they'

re so differ

ently-sourc
ed to envis

ion our liv

c) ing further

through them
We've only

ourselves

d) our life to

answer-for
our so other

wise-ways-of-
being-us.

One can't (3)

a) deny the color

ful flowering

s of this is
land's vast

b) palette of

charming

ly live-arti
facts They

keep renewing
our visual

c) and touch-

sense of The

Good Lord'
s creative-

presence.

Despite (4)

a) Israelis re

peated denial

of The Good
Lord's chosen

b) ness its eter

nal God remain

ed faithful
to his first–

beloved bring
ing it within

c) the essence

of His very–

being that re
deeming cruci

fixion for its
sins Yes millen

d) ia of that pain

ful operation

but at the end
"all's well

that ends well".

In Nomine
Domini
Cyprus October
13 2020

P. S. These wind- *(2)*

a) expansive

clouds open

ing-out
the heaven

s to their
Nielsen's

b) voiced "Expan

siva" 3rd sym

phony of al
most unlimit

ing timed-ex
posure

s.

Are cloud *(3)*

a) s heavenly-

sent messag

ing a pre–de
termining

future or

b) have they been

composed for
changeable

aesthetic–ap
preciation

or have they

c) languaged

as many ani
mals what still

remains pri
marily–inde

cipherable.

Clouding- *(3)*

a) over not only

protects from

the all-con
suming Cyprio

b) tic sun but

can help re

trieve shadow
ing remembran

ces of long-

c) forgotten

but still a
vidly express

ive once-upon-
a-time.

Are we leav (4)

a) *ing this is*

land defense

less against
its twice-

b) *timed occupy*

ing-Turks

The British
with their 2

airfield
s unlikely

c) *to defend*

The Greeks

no longer
existencial

ly-affected
Will we read

d) *even before*

our Diamond

Anniversary
in September

of its re-
occupation.

I imagine (2)

a) that the Brit

ish also an

islanded peo
ple know how

to better
cope with

b) those Cypriot

ic tide-change

able moon-im
pulsive poet

ic-imagin
ings.

Are these (3)

    a) Cypriotic

hills moving

as harmon
iously togeth

    b) er as Mozart

ean fluencie

s or do they
also impress

ion us with
immovable

    c) timelessly-

coherent

Haydnesque
architecton

ic–consisten
cies.

Poetry Book 106

Part 2

Other earlier Poems

If you're a (4)

a) woman with an

enthusiast

ic nature
you may rush

b) into serious

things like marr

iage and church
affiliation

one-eyed and
come-out with

c) more than just

burnt-finger

s Life may
have taken-its-

toll-on-you
but you've at

d) least thirsted

of its very-

essence in-
your-own-way

as complete
ly as possi

ble.

Dance of (2)

a) *Death It was*

one of the

lesser-leave
s twirling

-round as the
wind's most

b) *fancied-part*

ner but with

only a tiny
thin stem

holding it
short-timed

tight.

It became im *(4)*

a) portant for

me to know

whether he
said that in

b) dream or dur

ing our last

meeting to
gether When

dream and what

c) actually happen

ed become in
distinguish

able from one
another then

life itself'

d) s added another

dimension
to what could

have act
ually-happen

ed.

My curtain

s as my Rose
marie dressed

in a light
blue that such

days become
intimately

resolved in
heavenly and

earthly de
sign

s.

Our still *(3)*

a) blooming autum

nal–equinox

garden when
not inhabit

b) ed except by

its own flower

ed–blessing
s seems only

fully dress

c) ed when ap

praised by
our flower–de

signed presen
ce.

They needn't *(2)*

a) grace Corona

with a 2nd

chance She
took it on

her own encom

b) passing the

odds and end
s of what they'

d so long
failed-to-u

nite.

She'd had *(6)*

a) her bouts with

the evangeli

cals and then
with the Munch

b) ener Jesuits

but returned

(when she visit
ed us recent

ly) to the still

c) activating

church of her
christen

ing confir
mation and mari

tal vows Tradit
ional values

d) had replaced

her once so
high-lighted

enthusiasm
s. Had it

become misun

e) derstanding

s or too high
ly-levelled

expectation
s that left

f) her afterall

with but the

modest loneli
ness of her a

ging year
s.

Without a (3)

a) *biblically-*

oriented church

sermoned to
that blessed

b) *love of our*

Redeemer we'

d simply create
our own god

tailored to

c) *our own want*

s and need
s much as the

Church has
done ages–on–

end.

After 13 (3)

a) years of a

loving–togeth

erness they
finally decid

b) ed to get marr

ied not in a

church but
only official

ly recognized
(God only)

c) knows why)

something

like a sancti
ty of an earth

ly-sanction
ed-betrothal.

How far must (3)

a) one go to fully

empathise

with another'
s values and

tasteful-deter

b) mining-judg

ments There
must exist an

invisible
line between

relativis

c) ing one's own

life-support
ive views by

fully empath
ising with a

nother's.

She learned (3)

  a) the hard way

  how an other

  wise background
  could keep two

  b) persons apart

  from a sanctify

  ing middle-
  ground For some

  it's my way
  and none other

  c) wise she might

  become feared

  of losing her
  own self-secur

  ing ground-base.

Differing per (5)

 a) spective

s Why should

I see your
photograph

 b) s for their

own sake

when I'm most
especially

in need of

 c) discovering

what I and
poem require for

our book-sake
It's like a

d) choral conduct

or seeking-out

music not for
its self-signify

ing beauty's
but perhap

e) s for the limit

ed competance

of her over-
65-chorus.

Is this sky (4)

a) *actually two-*
faced the trans
parent contin
ually on-the-

b) *move cloud-pro*
cessional
and the other
wise spacious
ly unfathom
able blue Or

c) *does it repre*
sent an image
of our so-
called destiny
the coming and
going of histor

d) *ical phases and*
the ever-present
unfathomable
God-search
ing distance
s.

If the bible' (3)

a) s not God's

word or only

parts of it
that coincide

b) with our own

timely raison

d'être then
we're "lost

out here in
the stars"

c) without sense

and orientat

ion All that
in the adulter

ous name of
progress.

It may have (3)

a) *been hard to*

have not cho

sen such a
(self) valued

b) *father made*

somewhat more

palatable
by his more im

portant concern
s and a rebell

c) *ious elder sis*

ter While his

sanctimonious
way left him

not fully self–
defensible.

Ship of fools (8)

a)*Neil we're*

in the same
boat" at age

83 at the
height of our

b) *intellectual*

and artistic
powers rhythm

ically out at

c) *sea (I felt*

the waves tak
ing-hold of

our very-pre
sence) with

d) *those on-board-*

revelrie

s Yes I real
ised then The

e) Ship of Fools

far out beyond

reach of a
safetied re

turn home-
stay

f) for our dia

mond (60th)

anniversary
only a year

away as with
my mother's 105

g) th *birthday*

even personal
ly reserved

seats died be
fore it could

h) become celebrat

ing only a

ground–depth
ed funeral in

its time–expos
ing place.

First not (3)

a) yet fully

formed morn

ing light
as if raised

b) from the dark

on this early

autumnal day
will soon be

immensing

c) its brightly

sourced light
as leaf-in

voking death–
call

s.

He remained (2)

 a) personally

too nice (I

mean the bis
hop) to feel

comfortable
about quest

 b) ioning his so

humane and

tolerant
ly enlighten

ed church–
timed course.

Our dean *(3)*

> *a) here in Bavaria*
>
> who must-have-
>
> known of my
> vocal church–
>
>
> *b) exposing past*
>
> kept at arm'
>
> s length
> (not only be
>
> cause of Cor
>
>
> *c) ona) from his*
>
> new parishion
> er's danger
>
> ously expect
> ant-presence.

It's become (2)

a) our so frequent

ly across-the-

table's love-
embracing

most self-satis
fying eye-pledg

b) ed moments

daily renewing

a marriage
that still re

mains after 59
years so sens

ually-alive.

All's normal (3)

a) *for both-of-*

us on the

blood-recount
ing yearly-ex

b) *pectant med*

ical-front

that we've
cause on this

beauteous

c) *early autumn*

al day for an
especial togeth

erness-celebra
tion.

Women disap (2)

a) pointed in

love and/or

marriage (and
we've experien

b) ced several)

remain as the

American South
after the Civil

War somehow de

c) prived of what's

become dearest
for their own

raison-d'ê
tre.

That take-it (2)

a) or leave-it

attitude re

mains the
most reliable

defense for

b) sensitive

artists so
closely attun

ed to their
own creative-

presence.

Teaching *(3)*

a) in the most

Corona-necess

ary-way with
out personal

contact de

b) prives both

teacher and
student of

what's most
essential

for both that

c) receptive-

help in a de
humanizing

impersonal
oncoming-

world.

My two-sided *(3)*

a) reaction to

these oncoming

migrants As a
Christian here'

b) s the time and

placc to offer

them the spirit
ual comfort

s of a
faith-in-Christ

c) whereas a Jew

feared by their
Islamic endem

ic anti-semet
ism.

If Rosemarie (3)

a) *should die be*

fore me (what

I fear the
most) likely

b) *lack of a per*

manent home-

stay not of place
but personed

for a loneli

c) *ness of a lost*

long-timed to
getherness

identity-
cause.

If marriage (3)

a) *remains today*

simply as an

I-Thou relat
ion – One

b) *doesn't marry*

a family any

more as with
a German-Jew

relation

c) *freed as well*

from the haunt
ing shadow

s of an irre
pressible past.

If you listen (5)

    a) to the late

    Beethoven

    with a classi
    cally composed

    b) taste it might

    often sound

    (except for
    those great

    slow movement

    c) s) out-of-

    bounds from
    those carefully

    time-length
    exactly weight

d) ed works of

the late Haydn

and Mozart
New lands per

haps but hard

e) ly purveyed

by his perhap
s lesser-gift

ed successor
s.

Never having (4)

a) been a seaman

as Melville

I let those
tidal wave

b) s speak through

their awakened

distant sensi
bilities of

others Ocean

c) s time me in

a complete
ly different

way and mean
s from those

once-timed ex

d) plorers more

by their inex

tinguish
able sense-e

voking contin
uity.

One named *(3)*

a) Rains perpetu

ate differ

ing speeds and
flavouring

b) s They may re

main softly en

ticing scented
with sweet-

flowering

c) s as in summ

er or hard
and persistent

during late

d) autumnal cold-

spells but how
ever varied

we call them
simply rain.

These split- *(2)*

a) down roofs rare

ly accentuat

ed my way
They seem

b) nevertheless

to divide me as
well for an

impending un
known if for

eign and high
ly abstracting

cause.

With her (4)

a) One dare not

touch too–

closely to
her self-prim

b) ed sensibili

ties It hurt

s even before
duly express

ed as a child
defending its

c) first and per

sonally mine–

sensed puppet
Was Strindberg

rightly assess
ing "we hurt

d) what we love

the most" If

so I've done
it more than

I can realise
why.

An abandon (4)

a) *ed way that*

led into a

darkening
wood No one

b) *in sight that*

the echoing

of his seclud
ed steps es

tablishing

c) *a time and*

rhythm of
their own

until he knew

d) *they had stop*

ped confirm
ing his own

sense of voic
ed-being.

Why have mir

rors become
such an inti

mately person
al part of

self for a
woman dress

ed in her own
appealing i

dentity-cause.

Locked *(4)*

a) When we first

entered our

new home
22 Oak Lane

b) one small

door in the

down-staired
passageway

remained lock
ed No one

c) not even the

former owner

knew where
the key was

to be found
That locked

d) room became

for us in

time a mystery
of self-deter

mining length.

"*Just call (2)*

    a) me grandpa"

    that would

    help put-a–
    distance

    to that young

    b) talented pian

    ist from the
    jealous-eyed

    wife of a
    top-fit a

    ging-friend.

Two ways Two *(7)*

a) women both ro

mantically-
sourced marr

ied men with

b) a daily affin

ity for alco
holic drink

s Their love
would save

c) the husband

from dire-

straights
Naturally

they both

d) failed of

their enthu
siastic–cause

The one be
came relig

e) iously addic

ted to change

able faith-
causes but re

mained without

f) a stabilizing

future The o
ther also relig

iously-oriented

g) reared 4 child

ren of her own
down-to-earth

self-perpetua
ting future.

The children' *(2)*

a) world is

where some

poets and pain
ters discover

their own nat
urally sourced

b) need for what'

s remained of

their gen
uinely–naïve

spontaneous–
creativity.

Has poetry's *(4)*

a) become for him

and perhaps

for the late
Shakespeare

b) a means of

discovering

new island
s of distant

ly evocative-

c) callings or

a day by day
realising

of those un
touched trea

d) sures downed

from the sea'

s perpetual
ly aspiring

wave-length
s.

It usually (4)

a) comes abruptly

leaving us

little time
preparing

b) for the weath

ther's change

able season
s now plung

ing into
those fully

c) pfledged aut

umnal cooling-

off darkness
es the start

of that dy
ing phase of

d) the leave's dis

colored drift

ing-down death-
procession

als.

It remain (4)

a) s for me hard

ly imaginable

how Rosemarie
at age 82 man

b) ages to retain

much of her

fully-sourced
beautifying-

presence I

c) would perhap

s prefer be
lieving that

her always-lov
ing husband

d) has helped a

long that dia

loguing marr
iage timed-per

spective.

The American *(4)*

a) Pessoa didn't

achieve his e

qually astound
ing prolific

b) ness by creat

ing a four-per

soned perspect
ive rather o

therwise he

c) perspectiv

ed his daily
immensing poet

ic-output
through a sing

d) ular continu

ity of a deep

ly personal-
expressive

ness.

Compromise (4)

a) as the grand

American one
of 1850 only
achieves a

b) higher unity

of the compet
ing partie
s when its ap
parent aim be

c) comes equally

cherished
by both side
s Otherwise
now as then

d) civil war

will remain
constantly
poised–for
action.

Is the Japan (4)

a) *ese longevity*

with so many
of their eld

b) *ers over 100*

including the

oldest 118
still-alived

one caused by

c) *its fish espec*

ially raw-fish-
diet Though

such a one–

d) *sided interpre*

tation sound
s for a long–

confirmed his
torian a bit

fishy.

If keeping- *(2)*

    a) the-family-to

    gether had

    been a signifi
    cant role of a

    mother's be

    b) ing now

    feminised in
    to an other

    wise if strange
    ly-competing

    family-sense.

He as many *(4)*

a) Bavarian men

a live-or-

die FC Bayern
fan maintained

b) that soccer had

vastly changed

since the famed
Beckenbauer-

Müller days
faster and with

c) more bodily-con

tact I retorted

that the game
itself's become

more injury-

d) prone some

thing like A

merican football
a substitute

for war-like
activitie

s.

Do the hard- *(2)*

a) hats have hard

heads Or is it

just a pose
as with so

many men to

b) display their

so-called mas
culinity

for any inter
ested woman-

folk
s.

Handle-with *(3)*

a) care She's more

easily break

able than many
would realise

b) But that's

what makes

her particular
ly feminine

a continuing

c) pleasure for

one who's learn
ed through the

years to han
dle-with care.

For Hanni our (2)

a) photographer

If he could

be pictured
with Rosemarie

and his poetry-
pad that would

c) tell more-than-

enough of his

essential-be
ing reduced to

only two care
fully-chosen-

image
s.

The little (2)

a) next door boy

screeches

like a mouse
but in the

highest poss
ible register

b) and so intense

ly unnerving

my most arti
culately phras

ed poetic-de
meanor.

Fake or real (4)

a) Although he's

a Trump-first

er rather than
the America

first he claim
s to espouse

b) allowing till

now 200,000

Americans to
die from a not-

to-be-taken-ser
iously disease

He's also an

c) imitation-

Christian
posing with

his unused
bible in

front of a
church he doesn'

d) t attend But what

he has done

for unborn child
ren and for

Israel display
s a fighter-

first-courage.

These almost

impenetrable
fogs dissolv

ing in to the
hill's time-

consuming dark
nesses leav

ing behind
an impression

of rebirthed-
expectation

s.

Raw weather' (2)

a) s in dire straits

cold rains in

habiting this
restless un

ease as if

b) quietude

s and soften
ing expressive

ness had become
but foreign-

word
s.

Elgar's *(3)*

a) Pomp and Circum

stance still

somehow my
own slowly

rhyming pro

b) cessional

I'd gladly
share with Rein

er and Neil
as if time

itself had be

c) come intuned

to but an un
certained

steadfast pro
mising-fut

ure.

Torrential *(2)*

a) *rains inhabit*

ing most all

of our body'
s reclaimed

for safe–

b) *keeping now*

voiced with a
time–endur

ing if chill
ed expanding–

wetness.

Womanliness (3)

a) When does a

girl become

a woman cer
tainly not

b) through a

pre-timed bod

ied-competan
cy nor those

first advanc
es of puppy-

c) love Is woman

liness a kind
of attitude

perhaps of
self-compos

ure.

If I were a (3)

a) woman as my

two elder sis

ters I'd be
come quickly

b) sceptical of

men's decept

ive love-talk
and would

treat most of
them in a

c) motherly-fash

ion as one

does with over-
grown child

ren.

Most men be *(3)*

a) come equipp

ed with a

show-off nat
ure as in

those days

b) of authentic

chivalry They
love to per

form for the
assembled la

dies showing-

c) off their ta

lents as male
birds compet

ing for their
future nest-

maiden
s.

Poems or (3)

> *a) music for spec*
>
> ial occasion
>
> s rarely rise
> above express

> *b) ing just the*
>
> right kind of
>
> things for
> the birthday
>
> or whatever
> person duly

> *c) sanctified*
>
> and occasion
>
> ly as with
> Ingo with a
>
> rhymed–compe
> tancy.

Some person *(3)*

a) s usually of an

unusual aca

demic compet
ancy prefer

b) on special

occasion

s as my broth
er-in-law

Lee that stand–

c) off attitude

of critical
ly high-brow

ed word-re
straint.

A big cele (4)

a) bration Raphael

our retarded

son's 57th birth
day the room

b) quite small

packed with o

ver 20 person
s just as

the revelry be

c) gan he came

in death ex
posed bone-

sourced with
a look that

d) told us this

will be his

last-time-
together

ness.

These wind (3)

a) s seem now

wild-voiced

as if no
longer respon

sive to per

b) suasion of

any kind as
an adolescent

out-of-paren
tal-control

even of his

c) own well-be

ing without
message except

of that cha
otic no-man'

s-land.

Haydn's early *(3)*

a) violin concerti

possessed of

vital energy–
exposure

b) s leaving be

hind even be

fore they've
actually

started–off
destination

c) unnamed but

flighten

ly remain
ing uncertain

ed.

Bunched (2)

a) small yellow

flowers voic

ing a suspend
ing together

ness of what
they're try

b) ing to ex

press individ

ually reticent
ly awakening

to an orch
estral–conclu

siveness.

If at time (2)

a) s the eye has

become the

theme itself
the words

but a choic

b) ed selection

of why they
seem expand

ing beyond
their init

ial-impetus.

Wind-Phantom *(4)*

a) s The invis

ible wind makes

its presence
habitually

b) visible through

the swaying

of branches
its finely–

felt leaf-ex
posures even

c) heavenly

cloud-expan

sive But it
remains just

as habitually
silent to the

d) breath of

its secret

ly sourced–
message.

We didn't (5)

a) *Who would want*

to attend an

outdoor's Sun
day service

b) *with the grass*

fully wet-down

from the in
tense Satur

day rains and

d) *the sharp wind*

s at 45 de
grees That's

what we call
freedom Nothing

d) *secret nothing*

dangerous where

as so many
Christian

s today would
be supremely

e) satisfied

with the freed

om of such a
cool-wet Sun

day service.

Why I so (5)

a) often poetise

contradict

ary-behavior
I'm no mod

b) del for good

and correct

Judaic–Christ
ian behavior

That's one

c) reason why I

generally re
frain from

moralizing
But if any

d) one's such

an example

as only Jesus
Himself then

e) let him step-

forth and I'

ll be the
first to stand-

up to him.

If he's pre *(3)*

a) conceived and

treated in a

demonic way
he may in

b) time actual

ly grow horn

s and a char
acterist

ic tail and
maybe you'll

c) soon be mirror

ing his be

havior as if
really-for-the-

first-time.

Time's now (3)

a) in-a-hurry

It's not just

the wind's pre
vailing inten

b) sity or even

those cloud

s turmoiled
in unstead

ied gestur
ings but that

c) unease in one'

s blood in
creasing

ly pulsed–a
wareness

es.

Few painter (2)

a) s as Georges de

la Tour manage

to reconcile
their own

self-desiring
brush-stroke

b) to the im

pending still

ness of the
Christ Child'

s light-in
voking quiet

udes.

Our rather (2)

   a) old unused piano

   has in time

   quieted–down
   to at best a

   discussion–
   piece but one

   b) that rarely

   takes part in

   its self–fash
   ioned once Cho

   panesque awak
   ening finger

   ed–way
   s.

I can hard (2)

a) ly recognise

that bust of

me at age 6
Those eyes

do seem poet
ically enlight

b) ened but per

haps mirror

ing the sculpt
resses' slight

ly romantised
post–Barlach

ian way.

Each time (2)

a) I begin to

realise those

apples on our
look-out tree

seem to be
ripening

b) their round

ed-out reach

to the depth
of my own

eye's purpos
ing-intent.

Others as (4)

a) Richter and

Boccherini

may have writ
ten string

b) quartets be

fore Haydn but

no one except
perhaps Beeth

oven made that

c) highest of

instrument
tal forms

a continual
ly develop

d) ing innovat

ive personal

means of self–
expressive

ness.

How easily (4)

   a) our fortune

   s may change

   Those who be
   lieve in a

   b) so-called

   scientific

   means of fu
   ture develop

   ments should

   c) learn from

   Corona how
   quickly all

   such most–in

   d) teresting

   hypotheses
   become simply

   "gone with
   the wind".

Writing poem

(for Matthew and Andreas) (4)

a) s in many

ways resemble

s taking the
family dog

b) out for a

walk It know

s what it
wants and of

ten pulls us

c) that way but

there still re
mains a common

together
ness of en

d) joying the

spacial sniff

of fresh air
and a home-

based return-
trip.

That special (5)

a) *ly intense*

scent of

freshly-cut-
grass a pure

b) *delight for*

those who re

lish in such
an intoxicat

ing freshness

c) *but for other*

s it may re
lease running

noses a burn
ing-eye-feel

d) *ing and the*

desire to get

away as far
and as quickly

e) as possible

No two of us

are alike not
even "identi

cal" twin
s.

If animal' (2)

a) s behavior as

Aesop has pro

ven time and
again example

themselves
s for a moral

b) ising human-

type behavior

better than
the preacher'

s finger-point
ing pious-admon

ishion
s.

Why one must (2)

a) admit that

money-matter

s still re
main from one

driven-away
from such false

b) values

much-too-

high on
that unwritt

en list of exis
tencial-prior

itie
s.

Macke succeed

s most when
space become

s personed
in his over

all concept
of visual-si

lence
s.

Waiting' (4)

a) s a timed-

space all-its-

own waiting
for your lov

b) ed-one's

final yes or

no for the
child's 9

months timed–

c) expectation

s Waiting for
the doctor's

diagnosis
Waiting let

d) s us wait for

an other-timed

singular pur
posing-dia

logue.

The so under- (6)

    a) rated Altdorfer

    the greatest

    of German Renn
    aissance land

    b) scaping paint

    ers realising

    the still my
    sterious person

    alized quality

    c) of the not-so-

    darkening Eichen
    dorff's wood

    s Altdorfer with
    his unique epoch–

d) scope Altdorfer

the first to

conceive of a
pure landscape

completely for–

e) its-own-sake

Altdorfer the
anti–semite

responsible

f) for the Jews

being thrown
out of his

beloved Regens
burg.

Eve's little

bite with a
big big effect

has appled
us (if it

was an apple)
for centurie

s of self-en
during bond

age.

To-be-looked- (5)

a) at Something

s are simply

there to-be-
looked-at

b) for beauty-

sake or even

(un)histori
cally caused like

the soon-to-be

c) dismantled

monument
s thrown in

to the rag
ing seas of

d) their untimely

cause The beauty
of woman's speech

less composure

e) Art-for art's-

sake tastes my
senses at odd–

times quite-
similarly.

Judging art (4)

a) *through a pure*

ly secular

humanistic
point-of-view

of man's emanci
pating himself

b) *from the (un*

necessary) re

ligious connect
ion creating a

criticism at
odds with many

deeply relig

c) ious artists

Can one write
an entire book

on Moissac with
out realising

its fundament
al religious

d) ity And other

s whose lyrical

qualities es
tablish a guar

antee of their
poetic–affini

ties.

All in the (4)

a) name of progress

Is education

simply a matt
er of learn

ing what's

b) necessary

or is it also
a dialogical

means of char
acter-building

between the

c) classroom

teacher and
his or her

pupils Whereas
an impersonal–

digital–ab

d) stract-educat

ional–method
actually dehuman

ises the learn
ing-process.

If "my poetry' (8)

a) s better than my

self" then each

new dedicated
reader of my

b) verse estab

lishes a deep

er relation
to what's the–

better–part

c) of my essent

ial–being where

as friendship
s without

d) that better–

part–of–self

remain less–
substanc

ial? If my

e) ministerial-

self- establish

ing at least
2 decades of

my essential–

f) being were

to meet a
round the cor

ner my oncom
ing essential–

g) poetic-be

ing would they

have recognis
ed each other

h) or passed each

other by with

"you're not
really David

Jaffin".

Facts and fig (4)

a) ures can hardly

figure-out
why the way

ward winds

b) have sudden

ly changed
the direction

of your own
most intimate

c) inclination

s or why that

darkened pond
on the way to

the high school

d) seemed to depth

a still unknown
but irretriev

able poetic-
calling.

Reading my *(4)*

a) bookshelves

back to their

initial but
now somewhat

b) obscured im

petus is like

reading one'
s hands to dis

cover particu

c) lar charact

er–traits re
main hidden

from touch

d) and view only

to be reveal
ed while writ

ing–themselv
es–out.

The most un (3)

a) usually color
ed butterfly
which just
landed on my

b) sun-flourish
ing balcony
seems as if
it had been
guided

c) right then
and there for
my most appre
ciative aesthet
ic–instinct
s.

Women are *(3)*

> *a) so different*

ly made that

it's hard to
imagine that

> *b) all-of-them*

had been told

out of Adam'
s rib perhap

s rather to
indicate how

> *c) we've been*

called–togeth

er as one
perpetually–o
therwise-

self.

No one

could possibly
bring-togeth

er my collect
ed poems as

they recollect
themselve

s in to those
streams of e

lusive time-
telling.

After the (6)

a) first debate

It's expected

of an American
president

b) that he'll re

main mannered

enough not to
keep interrupt

ing his oppon

c) ent even the

moderator A pre
sident should at

least adhere
to the rules

d) of common de

cency But this

one obviously
considers him

above law and

e) order even bey

ond the expanding
realms-of-truth

Let's not for

f) get his role

model's still
firmly establish

ed on the 20-
dollar-bill.

Can one recog (5)

a) nise seasons by

their scent

Spring barely
scents its

b) first flower

ed awakening

s as if from
reticent dream

s The scent of

c) summer at the

height of its
activating sun

and heavenly
cloud-reach

d) Autumn's the

distant scent
of its inebria

ting fire
s whereas win

e) ter denies an

optimal scent

because of its
cold stand-

off appear
ance.

Did *(2)*

a) money

provide a safe
ty zone for

those Jewish finan
ciers protected

by the powers-
that-be or did

b) it create anoth

er source of

the mob's hate
and jealousy

just waiting
armed for the

next pogrom.

Pantheism *(2)*

a) 's whether Spin

oza's or Goethe'

s really no
different

than primitive

b) man's worship

of sun moon
stars and o

ther natural–
object

s.

Sometime *(4)*

a) s words slip

away willful

ly without
my poetical

b) ly stamped-

approval

out of my
mind's range

reaching un

c) attended

targets as
Word War II

bombs still
peacefully

d) underground

ed but then

a week ago
unexpected

ly exploded.

Having been (2)

a) intuitive

ly-warned of

unnecessary
words he cut–

them-down to
their essence

b) But that did

n't stop (not

for a single
moment) their

regenerat
ing-power

s.

Dog-walker (3)

a) s display

ing their own

character
as well hold

b) ing-tight

and tense

or letting
time-telling

c) free while

dogs answer

ing in their
own otherwise

doggish-way
s.

Why should (2)

a) *a non-Christ*

ian feel "a

sense of spec
ial security

through marr
iage" He could

b) *n't explain*

it to him

self but I
not his min

ister perhap
s sensed–the–

reason–why.

Poetry books by David Jaffin

1. **Conformed to Stone,** Abelard-Schuman, New York 1968, London 1970.

2. **Emptied Spaces,** with an illustration by Jacques Lipschitz, Abelard-Schuman, London 1972.

3. **In the Glass of Winter,** Abelard-Schuman, London 1975, with an illustration by Mordechai Ardon.

4. **As One,** The Elizabeth Press, New Rochelle, N. Y. 1975.

5. **The Half of a Circle,** The Elizabeth Press, New Rochelle, N. Y. 1977.

6. **Space of,** The Elizabeth Press, New Rochelle, N. Y. 1978.

7. **Preceptions,** The Elizabeth Press, New Rochelle, N. Y. 1979.

8. **For the Finger's Want of Sound,** Shearsman Plymouth, England 1982.

9. **The Density for Color,** Shearsman Plymouth, England 1982.

10. **Selected Poems** with an illustration by Mordechai Ardon, English/Hebrew, Massada Publishers, Givatyim, Israel 1982.

11. **The Telling of Time,** Shearsman Books, Kentisbeare, England 2000 and Johannis, Lahr, Germany.

12. **That Sense for Meaning,** Shearsman Books, Kentisbeare, England 2001 and Johannis, Lahr, Germany.

13. **Into the timeless Deep,** Shearsman Books, Kentisbeare, England 2003 and Johannis, Lahr, Germany.

14. **A Birth in Seeing,** Shearsman Books, Exeter, England 2003 and Johannis, Lahr, Germany.

15. **Through Lost Silences,** Shearsman Books, Exeter, England 2003 and Johannis, Lahr, Germany.

16. **A voiced Awakening,** Shearsman Books, Exter, England 2004 and Johannis, Lahr, Germany.

17. **These Time-Shifting Thoughts**, Shearsman Books, Exeter, England 2005 and Johannis, Lahr, Germany.

18. **Intimacies of Sound,** Shearsman Books, Exeter, England 2005 and Johannis, Lahr, Germany.

19. **Dream Flow** with an illustration by Charles Seliger, Shearsman Books, Exeter, England 2006 and Johannis, Lahr, Germany.

20. **Sunstreams** with an illustration by Charles Seliger, Shearsman Books, Exeter, England 2007 and Johannis, Lahr, Germany.

21. **Thought Colors,** with an illustration by Charles Seliger, Shearsman Books, Exeter, England 2008 and Johannis, Lahr, Germany.

22. **Eye-Sensing,** Ahadada, Tokyo, Japan and Toronto, Canada 2008.

23. **Wind-phrasings,** with an illustration by Charles Seliger, Shearsman Books, Exeter, England 2009 and Johannis, Lahr, Germany.

24. **Time shadows,** with an illustration by Charles Seliger, Shearsman Books, Exeter, England 2009 and Johannis, Lahr, Germany.

25. **A World mapped-out,** with an illustration by Charles Seliger, Shearsman Books, Exeter, England 2010.

26. **Light Paths,** with an illustration by Charles Seliger, Shearsman Books, Exeter, England 2011 and Edition Wortschatz, Schwarzenfeld, Germany.

27. **Always Now,** with an illustration by Charles Seliger, Shearsman Books, Bristol, England 2012 and Edition Wortschatz, Schwarzenfeld, Germany.

28. **Labyrinthed,** with an illustration by Charles Seliger, Shearsman Books, Bristol, England 2012 and Edition Wortschatz, Schwarzenfeld, Germany.

29. **The Other Side of Self,** with an illustration by Charles Seliger, Shearsman Books, Bristol, England 2012 and Edition Wortschatz, Schwarzenfeld, Germany.

30. **Light Sources,** with an illustration by Charles Seliger, Shearsman Books, Bristol, England 2013 and Edition Wortschatz, Schwarzenfeld, Germany.

31. **Landing Rights,** with an illustration by Charles Seliger, Shearsman Books, Bristol, England 2014 and Edition Wortschatz, Schwarzenfeld, Germany.

32. **Listening to Silence,** with an illustration by Charles Seliger, Shearsman Books, Bristol, England 2014 and Edition Wortschatz, Schwarzenfeld, Germany.

33. **Taking Leave,** with an illustration by Mei Fêng, Shearsman Books, Bristol, England 2014 and Edition Wortschatz, Schwarzenfeld, Germany.

34. **Jewel Sensed,** with an illustration by Paul Klee, Shearsman Books, Bristol, England 2015 and Edition Wortschatz, Schwarzenfeld, Germany.

35. **Shadowing Images**, with an illustration by Pieter de Hooch, Shearsman Books, Bristol, England 2015 and Edition Wortschatz, Schwarzenfeld.

36. **Untouched Silences**, with an illustration by Paul Seehaus, Shearsman Books, Bristol, England 2016 and Edition Wortschatz, Schwarzenfeld.

37. **Soundlesss Impressions**, with an illustration by Qi Baishi, Shearsman Books, Bristol, England 2016 and Edition Wortschatz, Schwarzenfeld.

38. **Moon Flowers**, with a photograph by Hannelore Bäumler, Shearsman Books, Bristol, England 2017 and Edition Wortschatz, Schwarzenfeld.

39. **The Healing of a Broken World**, with a photograph by Hannelore Bäumler, Shearsman Books, Bristol, England 2018 and Edition Wortschatz, Cuxhaven.

40. **Opus 40**, with a photograph by Hannelore Bäumler, Shearsman Books, Bristol, England 2018 and Edition Wortschatz, Cuxhaven.

41. **Identity Cause**, with a photograph by Hannelore Bäumler, Shearsman Books, Bristol, England 2018 and Edition Wortschatz, Cuxhaven.

42. **Kaleidoscope**, with a photograph by Hannelore Bäumler, Shearsman Books, Bristol, England 2019 and Edition Wortschatz, Cuxhaven.

43. **Snow-touched Imaginings**, with a photograph by Hannelore Bäumler, Shearsman Books, Bristol, England 2019 and Edition Wortschatz, Cuxhaven.

44. **Two-timed**, with a photograph by Hannelore Bäumler, Shearsman Books, Bristol, England 2020 and Edition Wortschatz, Cuxhaven.

45. **Corona Poems**, with a photograph by Hannelore Bäumler, Shearsman Books, Bristol, England 2020 and Edition Wortschatz, Cuxhaven.

46. **Spring Shadowings**, with a photograph by Hannelore Bäumler, Shearsman Books, Bristol, England 2021 and Edition Wortschatz, Cuxhaven.

Book on David Jaffin's poetry: Warren Fulton, **Poemed on a beach,** Ahadada, Tokyo, Japan and Toronto, Canada 2010.